HAGAR

FINDING LIGHT IN THE WILDERNESS

Patricia E. Darrah, Ph.D.

Sister Numee Publishing

Washington, DC

Dr. Hunt is a professor of counseling psychology, a licensed psychologist, and diversity consultant. In more than 30 years of experience, her private practice has been geared toward interpersonal, marital, and family relationships. She has provided diversity training to numerous corporations, schools, and municipalities. As an expert in post major trauma care, Dr. Hunt has provided professional services in the aftermath of the MOVE bombing in Philadelphia; aided corporate executives impacted by September 11; and assisted relocated survivors of Hurricane Katrina. Dr. Hunt is the executive director of the National Center for Family Recovery (NCFFR).

"And you will know truth, and the truth will make you free."

John 8:32 "NRSV"

PREFACE

This book is about finding the "light" (courage, wisdom, and understanding) while in a state of emotional "wilderness" (confusion, loneliness, and despair). The metaphors of "light" and "wilderness" were inspired by the biblical story of Hagar, an Egyptian slave-girl who lived nearly four thousand years ago. Hagar's traumatic life journey of enslavement in a strange land bears a striking resemblance to the lives of African American women who lived during and since the era of slavery in North America.

I unapologetically tell the story of Hagar with the sensitivity and empathy justly born of a conscious-minded descendant of slaves. The story of Hagar is laden with emotional trauma, as are the personal stories of my own wilderness experience, which I share in this book. My encounters with wilderness and light over many years have taught me that change is possible, especially when powered by faith and persistent effort.

Prior to learning how to tap into my inner light, I tried desperately to hide my feelings of confusion, loneliness, and frequent despair from everyone—in public, on the job, and at social gatherings. I wore a mask. When I stepped out of my front door I was in character; the role I played depended upon what I thought people expected. My emotional pain was so severe that I actually ached inside.

If you are suffering in the wilderness, I want you to know that you are not alone. The divine light of courage, wisdom, and understanding is within you. Just call on your inner light and remain open and receptive to the help it brings you. Your situation can get better; your light can glow brighter; and your suffering, along with your emotional wilderness, can fade away into the sea of forgetfulness.

The intent of this book is to reveal through the ancient art of storytelling how real-life wilderness experiences can have extremely positive outcomes. This is not to suggest that adversity is our only pathway to light; but it does have a successful track record for getting our attention, which is a necessary first step.

My heart is united with the messages of light that are conveyed in this book. Through quiet reflection and truth seeking, the words appeared, giving me insight; then another aspect of the light appeared, giving me the courage to write the words. I am truly humbled by the spiritual journey of writing this book, and I am enormously grateful.

When I first cried out in the wilderness of emotional pain and despair, it would never have occurred to me that one day I would write about my experiences. Publicly exposing my mistakes and missteps was inconceivable to me. These were secrets I planned to take to my grave…until they actually began to kill me. The truth has indeed set me free.

I am reminded of one of my most revered spiritual instructors, Rev. Ida Lee Childs, whom I once asked for advice concerning a sermon I was scheduled to deliver and had been stressing over. She calmly and with certainty said, "All you need to do, my child, is stand flat-footed and speak the truth." That is what I offer you in the pages that follow—my flat-footed truth.

Rev. Ida Lee Childs (1918-2007)
Former President of the Universal Hagar's Spiritual Church

"Arise, shine; for your light has come, and the glory of the Lord has risen upon you."

Isaiah 60:1 "NRSV"

INTRODUCTION

A Modern Day Prophet

Father George William Hurley (1884-1943)
Founder of the Universal Hagar's Spiritual Church

The story of how my grandparents became members of the Universal Hagar's Spiritual Church has been passed down in my family for six generations. I share this story in the order and simplicity of the African oral tradition in which it was told to me.

In the mid-1920's, my grandfather, Lewis Ferguson, who had recently migrated from Greenwood, South Carolina to Philadelphia, Pennsylvania, went with a friend to hear a lecture by a man called Prophet Hurley.

The Prophet's message had such a profound impact on him that he felt compelled to join the church that very night. When he got home, he immediately began to tell his wife

Mary, whom he called Babe, about the things Prophet Hurley had said. It all seemed to make perfect sense to my grandfather. He told my grandmother that the Prophet had explained that man (humankind) was spirit clothed in human flesh; heaven and hell were states of consciousness; Christ was the wisdom and power of God; and man could develop his innate spiritual powers through earnest study and scientific concentration.

Poppy, as his children called him, told Babe that Prophet Hurley intended to uplift the downtrodden masses of black people who had been freed from slavery a mere sixty years earlier. He said that the prophet talked of resurrecting the consciousness of the black race to its rightful state of equality among all the races of the earth. Poppy was ecstatic about Prophet Hurley's teaching that if we learn to think for ourselves, we can create what we desire. My grandfather then told his wife that he had joined the church that night. I never heard anyone mention my Methodist grandmother's immediate reaction to what she had been told. I did learn, however, that she joined the Hagar church soon after.

Both of my grandparents became church officers. They both were students in the Hagar's School of Mediumship and Psychology, and they both became life-long members of the Universal Hagar's Spiritual Association.

My mother followed in the footsteps of her parents, but my father remained a dedicated Baptist. All of my older sisters attended the Hagar church with our grandparents and mother. By the time my younger brother and I came along, my grandparents had passed away, but the Hagar church had become a strong family tradition.

I learned that the church was named for Hagar, a biblical character associated with the Genesis story of Abraham. The story is told that Prophet Hurley had a dream of a brown-skinned damsel who turned into an eagle. He identified the damsel as Hagar, and he interpreted the dream to mean that he was to establish a spiritual church for the purpose of uplifting the fallen humanity.

The prophet, who was later referred to as Father Hurley, established his metaphysically based church and named it for Hagar. A few years later, he founded the Hagar's School of Mediumship and Psychology—the most important aspect of his spiritual association.

My grandparents, my mother, six of her seven children, and one granddaughter graduated from the Hagar's School of Mediumship; and two of my mother's great-grandchildren are currently enrolled in the Hagar School.

The Hagar's Spiritual Church was primarily composed of black men and women who were the first or second generation of freed slaves. The empowering spiritual messages taught in the Hagar church created a new pride within its members. Many downtrodden blacks who had been taught that they were less than human flocked to hear the uplifting messages being delivered by the men and women who had been ordained by Father Hurley. Hagar preachers, like their spiritual prophetic leader, were not afraid to condemn post-slavery Jim Crow laws enacted to prevent blacks from receiving equal rights.

Hagar, a young girl taken from her homeland in North Africa and enslaved in a foreign land, was given a place of honor by a young black prophet who recognized her connection to his people. Hagar, the brown-skinned damsel who escaped into the wilderness and found light, was redefined by this young black prophet of the modern age. He introduced her to a recently unshackled race of black people as an iconic feminine figure who overcame her suffering by finding light in the wilderness. Hagar used the light of wisdom to move from maid to matriarch and deserves an honored place in history.

I am extremely proud of my grandparents for adopting a mode of worship that spoke against human injustice and promoted peace, equality, and acceptance of all people. I dedicate Hagar: Finding Light in the Wilderness to them in honor of their courage and wisdom in guiding our family toward a unique spiritual mode of worship. My connection with Hagar has developed over the course of many years. I still study and reflect upon her story with the intention of gaining greater understanding of the spiritual message related to wilderness and light.

Father Hurley passed away in 1943, only twenty short years after establishing the Universal Hagar's Spiritual Church Association. He left a legacy that has continued to uplift humanity for the past ninety years. The Hagar doctrine is offered to all truth seekers who are willing to do the required spiritual work.

Lewis Ferguson (Poppy) 1872-1934

Mary Watson Ferguson (Mommy) 1879-1940

"By three methods we may learn wisdom: First, by reflection, which is noblest; second, by imitation, which is easiest; and third by experience, which is the bitterest."

~Confucius~

CONNECTIONS

The Wilderness

"The wilderness" as a metaphor is used to describe a distressed state of mind resulting from previous unresolved traumatic life events. People who are said to experience emotional wilderness suffer from confusion, loneliness, despair, and many other painful emotions.

I suffered from early childhood trauma that resulted in feelings of sadness and low self-esteem. These wilderness symptoms were considered to be a normal part of my personality. Family members and teachers casually described me as having an overly sensitive personality. My third grade teacher even wrote on my report card that I was a good student but often "moody." I grew up wondering why I went from feeling good to feeling extremely sad for no apparent reason. Because my behavior was not disruptive, I was left alone to deal with my feelings. On the outside, I seemed to be fairly average or perhaps even better adjusted than many of my peers.

Carrying wilderness feelings inside will often cause repeated trauma as a result of a weakened ability to cope with the usual stress in life. Eventually, the individual may suffer from lingering or residual emotional effects that cause feelings of confusion, loneliness, despair, fear, rejection, anger, depression—and the list goes on. Extended periods of wilderness can result in addiction and/or suicide.

There are no age, gender, race, religious, social, or economic restrictions regarding who will experience the wilderness. Each individual has her own unique wilderness experience. No matter how many people share your life circumstances, only you can find the way out of your personal wilderness.

Whether you consider your personal wilderness experiences to be large or small does not really matter. You have the power within you to overcome any wilderness episode you encounter. Trust in the power that allows you to breathe without thinking and keeps your heart beating even when it feels broken. Trust that power, and you will experience the wilderness less frequently, and it will be less foreboding each time. You will survive the wilderness and live to laugh and be happy again.

The Light

The metaphor of "light," as used in this book, refers to our inner potential to develop courage, wisdom, and understanding. I focus on these three qualities because they played a tremendous role in helping me to understand the process of my own healing journey. Discovering the light is a magnificent, life-changing, and life-saving gift. The light appears when we have the courage to face our difficulties and the willingness to reflect upon our experiences. This type of self-discovery journey requires a great deal of honesty. In my case, it was extremely painful to reflect on the mistakes I had made and allow the shame and guilt to rise to the surface. I sobbed uncontrollably when I finally saw the truth of past events that I had denied for so many years.

The light is similar to a laser beam that goes deep under the surface and penetrates the bone to reach the truth. But not all of my revelations were painful. In fact, there were some instances of understanding that were relatively gentle, quick jolts. I was especially surprised when an insight came that was quite humorous. Yes, the light finally arrived that allowed me to laugh at myself. It took a few more wilderness experiences before I got to the point where I could handle others laughing at me, though!

Basically, what I am saying is that light (courage, wisdom, and understanding) is what guided me to seek and accept help. Like Hagar, my ancient female role model, I had run away into the wilderness of emotional despair and cried out to a power greater than my human self. The light came. My healing journey began, and it continues on a daily basis.

I am humbled and grateful for the life I live today. It is more than I ever expected while I was in the wilderness. Today, I expect all good to come to me. I expect a miracle and a blessing every day. There is no limit to what my inner light can do!

My life has changed because my thinking has changed. The light has given me wisdom to make better choices and understanding to have compassion for myself and others. Most importantly, I have developed the courage to share my experiences with the sincere prayer that someone who is suffering in the wilderness will read these words and decide to discover their own inner light.

The wilderness mind is still accessible to me if I choose to revisit it. But I do not. I affirm daily: "I choose LIGHT!" I look for the light in every situation. Do I still have wilderness feelings? Yes, but they come far less frequently and depart more quickly. The process evolves as I remain open and receptive to the lessons life offers me and the light that lives within me.

I suffered for an extended amount of time because I was good at pretending that everything was okay. My hope is that you will discover the light in the wilderness of your mind as soon as possible and begin to experience the joy, peace, and prosperity that are your birthright.

Hagar

If you are a woman or a girl in what has been called a "man's world," if you have ever felt misused, abused, abandoned, or betrayed, then you will feel kinship with Hagar. If you have ever run away or felt like escaping from an unbearable situation, you will relate to Hagar's story. You will relate to my story. If you have felt like a stranger in a strange land, or have been defined by others and assigned by them to a "lesser than" status in life, then you have experienced the wilderness and you will know Hagar. And you will understand me. Hagar's life will help light your pathway out of the wilderness of confusion, loneliness, and despair. That is what she did for me.

Hagar brings us the light of courage, wisdom, and understanding that brought her from slavery to freedom, and from maid to matriarch. Her story confirms that throughout thousands of years, from Hagar's day to ours, there has always been light in the wilderness.

And Hagar said, "...Have I really seen God and remained alive after seeing him?"

Genesis 16:13 "NRSV"

Not much is written in the Bible about Hagar. She is introduced in the middle of a story about a great patriarch—a man of God—and his beloved wife. Hagar is depicted as an "inferior" outsider whose role is to serve at the pleasure of her "superiors." As an African American woman, I know the weight of that expectation all too well. And as a woman raised in a church named for Hagar and dedicated to uplifting the downtrodden, I'd like to offer a slightly different perspective on the story.

Hagar was likely too young to give voice to her circumstances, but old enough to harbor the trauma of separation from her family and African homeland. She was taken to a foreign land, enslaved, and given by her master to his wife as a handmaid. Living in the tent of her mistress provided Hagar a protected status among her master Abram's followers. His selection of Hagar to be the personal maid of his beloved wife Sarai suggests that he recognized Hagar's superior traits.

I imagine that Hagar eventually grew accustomed to the language, food, clothing, and religious rituals of Abram and his people. She also must have learned to eventually accept the perpetual feelings of "otherness" that exist in the hearts of those devalued for their differences.

Hagar was a slave-girl and a maid, not by birthright or personal choice, but by forced assignment. I suspect that her work was less difficult than the labor of other slaves, yet she surely felt just as bound. It is possible that she survived her adverse circumstances by embracing the treasured memories of her early childhood. The fact that Hagar was chosen as a handmaid to Sarai suggests that she was well bred. And the people of her native land (Egypt) were deeply spiritual. Her experience in the wilderness is indicative of a deep-rooted faith that must have been instilled long before her captivity.

Hagar was, no doubt, growing into a graceful and attractive young woman. Her mistress Sarai, noticing Hagar's budding maturity, saw potential for using the slave-girl to fulfill a personal desire. Sarai was barren and deeply saddened that she was incapable of bearing a son for her husband. She arranged for her husband to go into the tent of her handmaiden so that through Abram's seed, Hagar could give him a son to be his heir.

I envision Hagar as healthy and strong, and it probably did not take long before she became pregnant, glowing with a rounded stomach that revealed the development of Abram's seed. She was carrying the child of the respected leader of his people. I believe that Hagar could have found in this new situation an opportunity to recapture her freedom and reclaim her diminished sense of value.

The time Hagar spent with Abram must have been difficult for her at first. But the Bible depicts Abram as an understanding and faith-centered man. I imagine that he was quite interested in hearing stories about her country, and that Hagar felt honored to share with him all that she remembered about her family, homeland, and the culture of her people. Perhaps Hagar even hoped that her unborn child would someday know the beauty and grandeur of her African homeland.

Hagar's growing self-esteem and blossoming fertile body did not go unnoticed by her mistress. Sarai perceived Hagar's uplifted spirit as an air of superiority. She quickly sought to return Hagar to an acceptable attitude of servitude. In order to fulfill her goal, Sarai began to treat Hagar harshly. Hagar was not used to receiving such cruelty from her mistress, and she soon found Sarai's punishments unbearable. I believe that Hagar entered a mental state of loneliness, confusion, and despair. She had entered the wilderness of her mind before she ever fled into the physical wilderness.

The biblical story tells us that Hagar ran into the wilderness to escape the harsh treatment of her mistress. In a place of despair, Hagar summoned the faith that was passed down to her by the ancestors and shared with her long ago in her African homeland. It was faith that gave her hope that her tears and pleas for help would be heard in the wilderness. This act of asking for help and revealing her vulnerability was an act of courage. Although no physical being was there to hear her, Hagar's action brought forth the wisdom and understanding that only come from higher consciousness—the place where guiding angels reside.

Hagar knew that God had heard her cry for help. Calmness overcame her, and she began to hear an inner voice that foretold her future. Hagar's experience was so profound that she said, "Have I really seen God and remained alive after seeing him?" (Gen. 16:13 NRSV).

Hagar was guided to return to her mistress with an attitude that would protect her and her unborn child. The inner voice that she understood as truth had assured her that she would give birth to a healthy son. Hagar's revelation also foretold that God would multiply her offspring so greatly that the multitude could not be counted. This meant that she and her son would be blessed with abundant prosperity. This is the same promise that God made to Abram.

I imagine that Hagar knew from her inner communication with God that she and her son Ishmael would have to face future adversity before reaching their promised destiny. Even if she did not know where the faith to believe these new thoughts came from, she knew in her heart that they were true.

Hagar left her state of wilderness and returned to face the circumstances of her life. She resumed her daily chores with an intentional humility that pleased Sarai and brought their relationship back to the familiar status of mistress and maid.

As time passed, Sarai and Hagar regained some of the comfort that existed in their earlier relationship. I believe both women must have experienced excitement and anticipation as the birth of Abram's heir approached.

The day that Hagar gave birth to her son, Ishmael, she must have been blessed with the joy and celebration befitting the long awaited heir of Abram. Both Sarai and Abram treated her kindly as she nursed the son that they had long awaited. Life for Hagar and Ishmael remained pleasant as Abram and Sarai enjoyed the role of co-parenting and watching Ishmael grow. It appeared that all past transgressions had finally been forgiven and perhaps forgotten.

Years passed, and Abram's son was approaching the age of thirteen. According to Hagar's Egyptian culture, her son was about to become a man. The ritual of his journey to manhood included circumcision, and Hagar had shared this religious rite with Abram in preparation for the important event. Abram's decision not only to allow Ishmael to be circumcised but to include himself and all of the males among his people in the ritual was an extraordinary sign of Hagar's influence. For Abram, the act was symbolic of his covenant with God. It ushered both him and Sarai into a higher spiritual connection that led to their name changes. They were now to be called Abraham and Sarah, which represented that God's hand was in their lives.

Some time following Abraham's circumcision, to the astonishment of everyone, Sarah became pregnant. She gave birth to Abraham's second son, Isaac. Abraham's family remained content as his people grew in faith and size under his leadership.

After several years, Sarah saw that her son Isaac was healthy and able to survive their difficult desert lifestyle. She became concerned that Hagar's son, being the first-born, would be heir instead of her own son Isaac. Sarah complained to her husband Abraham that it would not be right for the son of the slave-girl to be heir instead of her son. She would not rest until Abraham reluctantly agreed to send Hagar and his first-born son Ishmael away.

Disenfranchised and abandoned, Hagar found herself once again in the wilderness of confusion, loneliness, and despair. This time, she was a single mother whose son was near death from hunger and thirst. Hagar became frantic and ran back and forth in the desert looking for water to save her son's life, never imagining that history would later uphold and imitate this passionate action as the ultimate reminder of her covenant with God. She cried out in the wilderness for divine intervention, remembering that she had once before found light in the wilderness.

As the story goes, a sense of calmness once again engulfed Hagar. She looked at her son breathing weakly under a nearby tree. She saw what appeared to be water at the heel of his foot. Hagar rubbed her eyes and looked again. She walked over and placed her hand on the ground and felt dampness. She began to dig with her hands and the clear water flowed upward from the dry ground. She filled her empty water skin and slowly quenched the thirst of her son. Hagar saw him reviving just like a withered plant being nourished by a long overdue rainfall. Hagar then drank from the sack and felt her own energy being refreshed.

A bright light appeared before Hagar, and she was reminded of her previous wilderness experience when the spirit of God appeared to her. She remembered that her son was destined to be a great leader. Hagar looked into the light and saw a prosperous and joyful future for herself and her son.

Hagar's wish that she would someday take her son to her beautiful homeland was fulfilled. After he became a man, she took Ishmael, who was now a wealthy and respected leader, to her homeland to find him an Egyptian wife. Hagar was now the respected matriarch of her family. They who were cast out were now fruitful and produced offspring of royal status. All of those beautiful visions that had appeared to Hagar had been fulfilled. She gave thanks to the God who had seen her suffering and appeared to her.

Hagar's powerful spiritual awakening in the wilderness is a testimony that encourages us to seek light in the wilderness. Hagar went from slavery to freedom and from maid to matriarch. She is an ancient feminine symbol of our ability to ask for light (courage, wisdom, and understanding) and overcome the wilderness (loneliness, confusion, and despair).

Hagar, The woman who saw God, gives us a proven pathway to overcoming our suffering.

The short testimonies in the pages that follow are offered in honor of Hagar. Those of us who have witnessed light in the wilderness must speak to the hearts of those who still suffer.

I Am Hagar

My spirit passes through the ages
   Entering your higher consciousness
I have chosen you to walk with me
   Daughters of my image
I will show you the greatness of your ancestors
   And you will remember them
I bring you courage, wisdom and understanding
   To overcome your suffering
Be proud and walk in dignity
   For you are of royal blood
Some try to steal me from you
   Try to hide me from your sight, but they fail
Because I am there in your mind's eye
   Ever present
Feel me now my daughters
   As I vibrate through your soul
 I am Hagar

~by Patricia E. Darrah~

"When you are sorrowful look again in your heart, and you shall see that in truth you are weeping for that which has been your delight."

~Kahlil Gibran~

HONORING MY FEELINGS

My sister Essie was the light in my earliest wilderness experience. I was five years old and excited about attending school for the first time. Kindergarten would be a whole new world for me, and there was joyful anticipation in the air. My big sister, Essie, combed and braided my hair in a special-day style. I was bathed, dressed, and eager to walk hand-in-hand with Essie the few blocks to our neighborhood school.

Finally, I was there in what seemed to be a huge classroom, surrounded by lots of excited children, chairs made especially for tots like me, toys that I had never seen before, and a friendly white lady who said she was the teacher. All of the children were Negroes, as we were referred to in 1949, but the teachers were mostly white. This was not a surprise to me because I was used to seeing white people in my community. The grocer at the corner store, the insurance man who came to our house every week, and the lady who ran the bakery on another nearby corner were all white. The teacher told us that we could play as she, Essie, and other parents watched. Essie was nearly fourteen years older than me and had taken on the role of surrogate mother for me while my mom did domestic work in the homes of middle and upper class white families. I respected Essie; I was obedient to her and thought of her as a younger mommy figure. I was used to Essie taking care of me. My mother was forty years old when I was born and had raised five daughters before me. They all helped out when needed, but Essie was single, lived at home and did not have a job due to her health problems. She became my primary caregiver in my mother's absence. Taking care of me was a role Essie seemed to enjoy. We had a very special relationship; she gave voice to my feelings. I do not recall any other adult asking me how I felt or what I thought. It was later in life that I understood that Essie had implanted in me the idea that what I thought and felt mattered. In those early years, such an idea was not easily accepted; it was generally believed that children should be seen and not heard. I abided by that rule most of my childhood.

I was happy to be at school. Essie had told me that school was fun and that I was very smart and would be a good student. Her words led me to believe that school was going to be a place where I would be happy. Her words also became prophecy, because institutions of learning became environments that nourished the shy Negro girl, the resentful colored teenager, the self-determined black young adult, and the spiritually and intellectually inspired African-American womanist that is me.

When the teacher told us to line up, I listened and obeyed. I knew that it was important to be a "good girl" in school. I was proud of myself. Later, it came time for Essie to talk with the teacher. I heard the teacher explain that due to crowded conditions and the fact that my birthday was not until January, I would have to wait a term before entering kindergarten. My heart sank. I experienced my first rejection—a disappointment that would become my earliest wilderness memory.

My big sister held my little hand, and we walked down the street toward home. I did not utter a word, but my little heart was broken. How could such joy be denied me? I searched my five-year-old ego-centered brain to find where I might have fallen short. In my world, if I did not get what I wanted, it must be because I was not good enough. It's sad to know that many children, if not taught otherwise, will blame themselves when so-called "bad things" happen to them. Perhaps I had gotten the idea that I was not enough when my baby brother was born. I was only one and a half years old when I had to give up my seat on my mother's lap. Giving birth to a boy after having six girls was a joyous event for my parents. I was baby girl number six, and he was the first boy and the youngest child. I don't recall how early I got the message that he was special, but I definitely got that message. Unfortunately, I also got the message that I was just another girl. This is the only explanation that might account for my early feelings of rejection that usually rendered me silent.

Being turned away from kindergarten was my first clear memory of an "I must not be good enough" moment. Essie said, "It's okay, Patty. You'll get to stay home with me a while longer, and we'll have fun." She stopped at the corner candy store and bought a bag of spearmint leaf candies. She plopped one in my mouth, and as my taste buds burst with the sweet, juicy delight, Essie assured me that I would start school soon and I would do just fine in the meantime.

I felt better, much better. Not just because of the sugary treat that still filled my mouth, but because someone had noticed my feelings, honored them, and comforted me. I was important! My feelings mattered. Essie's encouraging words paired with the sweet and chewy candy in my mouth provided me with an intrinsic awareness that such a combination could soothe my emotional pain. I would use this convenient remedy to escape the confusion, loneliness, and despair of many future wilderness experiences. Essie's gentle and caring words became the light in this early wilderness experience. Even though I did not understand it at the time, my memory of Essie would help me to find the light in the wilderness many times along my life journey.

I did start school the following term, and Essie escorted me there and picked me up in the afternoon. She was my rock. She was the one who saw my hurt and comforted me. Essie was the big sister that was most often nearby when I fell and skinned my knee or felt rejected by my playmates. She would talk to me and she would listen to me. When Essie combed my hair or dressed me, she would ask my opinion about how I looked. Her involving me and asking about my feelings felt good. It made my relationship with her special and has kept her forever in my memory.

Just a couple of weeks before Essie's twenty-first birthday, she died. Her heart had been damaged by rheumatic fever when she was a child. The day Essie died, I lost the one person who saw and acknowledged my pain. I was seven years old, confused, lonely, and in despair. I would carry the wilderness of Essie's death with me for many years.

Just as I had not uttered my disappointment after my postponed kindergarten start-date, I did not share my hurt with anyone over my sweet sister's death. I cannot recall my parents nor any of my siblings talking about losing Essie. Our home was dark and quiet for a long time following Essie's death. We must have all been grieving privately and painfully.

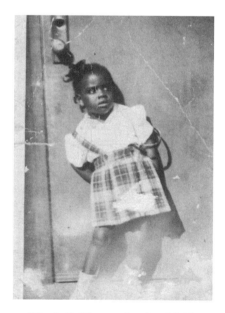

"Patty" (the author) - 1948

The Wilderness

It was not the story itself that led me into the wilderness; it was what I thought and believed about the story that guided my behavior. I cried alone many nights because I believed that I was unworthy of the love and kindness that Essie had provided. In the weeks following Essie's death, I would lay in bed staring at the ceiling. Warm tears ran across the sides of my face, caressing the curves of my ears, and finally dripping onto my pillow. I whispered, "Essie please come home. Please, please come home." I promised God that if he would let Essie come home, I would always be a good girl. I missed her, and I saw no other outlet to express my sadness. I could hear my mother tearfully praying in the bedroom next to mine. I imagined that she, too, was asking God to send Essie back home.

The sorrow I experienced over Essie's death taught me, at the tender age of seven, that there was a type of pain beyond my childish imagination. No skinned knee, busted lip, or sprained ankle could ever compare to the excruciating emotional suffering of too many restless nights. Essie never returned home. Either God did not hear me, or He did not care. Either way, I felt that I was powerless. This meant to me that I alone must protect my feelings. I covered my pain with a familiar blanket of silence. I learned that loving and needing someone could lead to pain and suffering. I needed to be careful not to let people, anyone, become so close that losing them would cause me such suffering. I never shared my thoughts or feelings with my parents or sisters. They probably thought that I was too young to really understand or feel what they were feeling. I am sure that my silence led them to believe that I was okay. I was not okay! Essie's death, for me, was a devastating, traumatic event. I thought that I must have been unworthy of her love, kindness, and encouraging words. Why else would God have taken her from me? These thoughts of unworthiness kept me in a state of chronic wilderness for many years. The slightest indication of criticism or rejection caused me to retreat into a state of self-blame, self-degradation, and self-hatred. It was all my fault. I wasn't good enough. I needed to try harder to be good, acceptable, and worthy. I was not okay, but I would not know that until later in my life.

Most likely, I appeared to be normal to the casual observer because I was always trying to be good. One observant elementary school teacher did, however, comment on my report card that I could be "moody" at times. Her remark was no doubt taken as an attitude or behavioral issue. Even she probably did not view it as a sign of childhood trauma.

During the second and third year following Essie's death, positive things began to happen that lifted my self-esteem. I joined the Girl Scouts of America, and my academic performance started to improve. However, before I could become grounded in this new sense of well-being, my world abruptly changed again.

The new medium of television entered my home and violently affirmed that I was, indeed, unworthy. Sitting in my living room, I stared at the small round television screen and watched governors and senators of the United States of America say that they would die before little Negro girls like me went to school with their white children. No white person had ever said anything mean to me before, so I was shocked. I had been called ugly and black (meaning that my complexion was dark) by a few children at school, but light skinned children were also attacked and called yellow in a derogatory manner. But these people on television were adults, and they sounded as if they hated Negroes of all ages and complexions.

I was afraid and angry at the same time. Worst of all, they were robbing me of my budding sense of self-confidence. It was 1954, and I was ten years old. I felt frightened by these authority figures spewing hatred in the streets of America and through the television screen.

A wilderness of confusion, loneliness, and despair surrounded me, as I held onto feelings of sadness, anger, and fear for many years. The childhood traumas I had suffered were less critical than those many children had endured; yet my emotional wounds were deep and festering inside. I longed for relief from the burden of hiding my true feelings. In a chronic and recurring state of suffering, I once again sat alone in my room, crying. I had reached a point of exhaustion, so I cried out from the depths of my soul for help. Inadvertently, I had taken my first step toward the light by admitting to myself that I needed help. Following that moment of pure emotional vulnerability, I felt a sense of relief. A glimmer of hope entered my mind and focused my attention toward the light and away from the wilderness.

The Light

My attention was drawn to people who dared to express their feelings. I became fascinated by real and fictional characters who spoke their truth. One day, I thought, I will be able to tell people the truth of what I think and feel. Reaching that goal became my avocation. Simply learning to recognize and identify my feelings was a journey of expanding fulfillment. I read self-help books that encouraged emotional expression. My self-awareness grew. Frequent practice helped me to gain needed self-expression skills. I would mimic the words of others who stated their feelings with comfort and ease. I recall a co-worker who, when displeased with something, would preface her remarks by saying "I'm not comfortable with…." Her preamble seemed to get and keep the attention of others.

She honored her feelings, and people listened to her words. Stating my feelings up front became a strategy that helped me to be aware of what I was feeling. I learned to say, "I feel" instead of "I am." Somehow, it helped me to take ownership of my feelings without making them an unchangeable aspect of myself. Feelings come and go, but what "I am" reflects a permanent condition or state of being.

When I was in a situation that triggered emotional discomfort, I would try to express how I felt to someone. My feelings had been buried for so long that I sometimes misinterpreted them. For example, I might say that I felt sad when I was actually feeling angry. I later learned through the study of psychology that sadness or depression was anger turned inward.

My intellectual abilities were strong, but my emotional growth was still in its infancy. Early attempts at verbalizing my feelings were often awkward. Once I asked someone to tell me her true feelings about a short essay I had written. When she offered her criticism of my work, I unexpectedly started crying. I was embarrassed and unable to offer an explanation for my behavior. I believe that my response upset her. She rather abruptly told me that I should not ask for feedback I could not handle. I remember at first thinking how insensitive she had been. But later I thought how amazing it was that she was able to express her feelings and speak her truth despite my tears. She also imparted a valuable lesson: I needed to learn more about my vulnerabilities before attesting to my ability to withstand criticism. Learning to honor my feelings meant that I would need to give them time to heal from many years of distress. I continued to take baby steps, and eventually my ability to express my feelings increased and my anxiety decreased. I had a long journey ahead of me with the ordinary ups and downs of life. There would be setbacks and future challenges, but at least I knew that I, like Hagar, could find light in the wilderness.

Hagar was separated from her Egyptian family and suffered just as I had with Essie's death. I imagine that she, too, cried alone many nights over the loss of her loved ones. Similarly, Hagar suffered the emotional anguish of discrimination and debasement in the land where she resided. My emotional connection to Hagar is evident to me. Although she lived thousands of years ago, her spirit spoke to me. It clearly encouraged me to find light in the wilderness.

Reflecting back on my responses to racism and to Essie's death, I realized that there was always light in the wilderness of those experiences. The ordinary people that risked their lives, standing up, sitting-in, and marching for freedom demonstrated the light of courage by bravely expressing their discontent. When I read or listened to messages of peace, reconciliation, and forgiveness, I encountered the light of wisdom. And whenever I thought about Essie's kindness and sensitivity to my feelings, I was embraced by the divine light of understanding.

My journey to honor my feelings has allowed me to honor and respect the feelings of others. I especially have a great sensitivity toward children. In my adult years, I have made an effort to listen to children, like Essie listened to me. I compliment them often, take notice of their various expressions, and attempt to get them to express their feelings. I have an eight-year-old great nephew who has an amazing capacity to express his feelings. His emotional vocabulary often surprises his teachers and other adults. I beam with joy whenever he speaks his truth. I like to believe that I have played some small role in helping him develop his magnificent gift of self-expression.

My own healing journey of honoring my feelings continues, but the difference between the past and present is like night and day. I am growing in understanding that even in the darkest wilderness, there is always light.

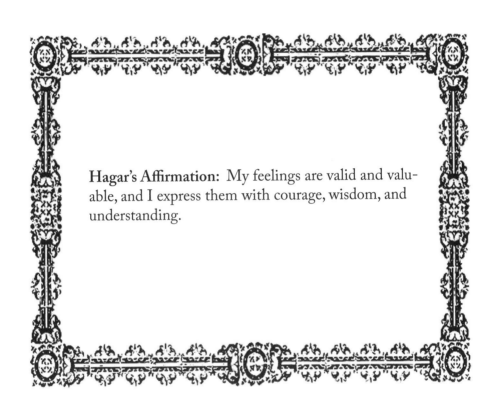

Hagar's Affirmation: My feelings are valid and valuable, and I express them with courage, wisdom, and understanding.

"Whatever someone did to you in the past has no power over the present. Only you give it power."

~Oprah Winfrey~

SEEKING HELP

My sister Zorah taught me how to be a lady. She was smart, attractive, soft-spoken, and a gifted seamstress by avocation. Most of all, she was cultured. I'm not sure where she learned her upper-class values and mannerisms, but she had them. Zorah was very kind to me without being "touchy-feely." She bought and made me beautiful little dresses and took me downtown for lovely cultural events. We saw live stage plays and museum exhibits, and we shared hot chocolate and cinnamon toast at the elegant tea room of an upscale department store. Sometimes Zorah and I would just walk around center city taking in the sights, and before catching the bus back home, she would treat me to a huge vanilla ice cream soda at the counter of Woolworth's Drug Store.

The places Zorah took me were predominately populated by whites until we showed up, better groomed and dressed than most in attendance. This was in the early to mid 1950s, so in a manner of speaking, Zorah and I were doing our part to integrate public facilities, albeit in the North. Zorah always seemed to act as if she were the most important person in the room, and I mimicked her behavior. I loved Zorah! She was the big sister that spent the most time in the household as I grew up. She never married or had children, but she helped to rear me and many other children during her eighty-year life span. Before Zorah made her transition from this earthly existence to her spiritual home, I had demonstrated the positive effects of her influence by completing graduate school and becoming financially self-sufficient and able to help others. I loved being helpful. Perhaps I needed to feel appreciated; I was one child among seven and it was easy to feel overlooked.

Zorah, this wonderful, generous lady who was my big sister, also played a major role in my childhood wilderness. Zorah was a great role model for me in many ways, but she also had another side. A part of Zorah remained a secret to me for my entire childhood. She suffered with paranoid schizophrenia, and I was often a target of her delusional fury.

I sat crouched in shock and fear on the landing of the dark cellar steps. The huge coal-burning furnace roared on and off like it was a fire breathing, child-eating monster waiting for me to reveal my location. I sat silently, heart throbbing, arms wrapped around my knees, eyes closed, too afraid to cry. Here I was in a terrifying wilderness, alone and confused, not understanding why I had been grabbed by my arm and tossed into the darkness. Zorah was angry with me. She raged in a barely audible voice, "You little dirty slob, stay in there until your mother gets home!" What had I done? My fate must be due to some failure on my part to be lovable, or so my eight-year-old brain told me. I balled up my little fists and began hitting myself in the face, muttering, "Ugly, ugly, dirty, slob!" I stopped when I became tired; I suppose it was my way of releasing the negative energy and fear that engulfed me. Then I just sat quietly waiting to be rescued, which always happened, sometimes even by Zorah herself. I have no memory of any of my rescuers saying anything more to me than, "Go upstairs to bed," or, "go outside and play." I believe that the adults in my life did not perceive the treatment I suffered as abuse, since they did not see any physical harm and I never complained. Therefore, the idea of abuse probably never entered their minds. This lack of knowledge regarding emotional abuse was quite common in the 1950's. I was an adult before I shared any of my wilderness experiences involving Zorah with a confidante or a professional therapist.

The last time Zorah ever treated me harshly was when I was about twelve years old. I was lying in my bed asleep, when suddenly the ironing board came slamming down on top of me. I woke up to find Zorah standing at the foot of my bed, trying to yell. Her voice always lost its volume when she was upset. I had forgotten to put the ironing board in its proper place, and I accepted her behavior as the result of my youthful irresponsibility. I had grown used to the regiment and quietly got up and took the ironing board to its appropriate place. "A place for everything and everything in its place" was Zorah's motto. My body ached from the ordeal, but I thought that it was my fault for forgetting to be neat. I never blamed Zorah; she was my loving, kind, big sister. Intuitively, I knew that these explosive episodes were not coming from the true Zorah, the Zorah who loved and pampered me with life's finer things. Perhaps my praying mother knew about Zorah's other side, but we never discussed it. The only indication that someone else knew about "the other Zorah" was when one of my aunts said, "Zorah is sensitive," in a secretive whisper.

During my teenage years, Zorah introduced me to word games, tennis, biking, hiking, and thinking about others with compassion. It was not until I was nineteen years old that I found out that Zorah had been diagnosed with paranoid schizophrenia. In my early adulthood I studied psychology, and I remain convinced that she also suffered severely from obsessive compulsive and anger disorders. What I do know is that the light seemed impossible to see during those childhood wilderness episodes. My positive and negative experiences with Zorah left me in a wilderness of confusion. I loved and enjoyed my activities with my big sister, and yet I was afraid of her unexpected outbursts of rage. The effects of my relationship with Zorah led me into a cycle of self-inflicted wilderness experiences.

The Wilderness

My periodic experiences of childhood emotional abuse ended when I was around twelve years old. The emotional residue of those experiences became an integral part of how I interacted with others. My life journey, prior to dealing with the impact of my childhood trauma, was filled with painful wilderness experiences. I desperately sought approval in all of my relationships in order to feel safe.

During my teens I was easily hurt by a mere comment of disagreement or dissatisfaction, no matter the source. If a teacher said anything other than excellent, I felt degraded. If a friend or acquaintance mentioned some small imperfection in what I said or did, I would be devastated. But all of these feelings and thoughts were kept buried deep inside. After all, it would have been "improper" to react negatively. It must have been my fault and I must be the one to fix it. This was an awful lot for a young person to bear.

The lessons that I had mis-learned from my childhood abuse were that: I would be punished for doing anything wrong;; it was my fault; if I was a "good girl" bad things would not happen; and nobody is going to deal with what happens to me. These mis-learnings rendered me emotionally unable to be comfortable in my own skin. I put forth enormous effort to be kind to others, to be obedient to adults, and to gain favorable feedback by being helpful. I longed for the immediate "thank you" that came from someone I had helped. It was no coincidence that my middle- school graduation class voted me "Most Helpful." I welcomed this positive recognition of my eagerness to be helpful. However, I later grew to understand this "documented" award was an early unofficial diagnosis of co-dependence. My unrelenting search for approval drove me deeper and deeper into states of untreated chronic depression. It was impossible to please all of the people all of the time. No matter how hard I tried, I fell short. Feelings of confusion, loneliness, and despair surrounded me in a self-perpetuated state of wilderness.

By the time I reached my late twenties, I could no longer hide my suffering. Alone in my apartment, I cried out into the darkness for help. Without sharing my despair with anyone, I had survived betrayal, rape, abortion, broken relationships, and attempted suicide. Finally, I was willing to surrender. I sincerely and humbly cried out in the wilderness for guidance. I wanted the suffering to stop. In the wilderness of confusion, loneliness, and despair, I asked for peace. A surprising calmness came over me. My crying stopped, and I fell into a restful sleep.

The Light

I awoke with a new sense of hope and determination to make changes in my life. Perhaps I had reached such a low point emotionally that there was no place else to go but up. I needed to relieve my suffering, but I had no idea what to do.

While I was attending college, my psychology professor was very kind to me when my emotional instability caused me to consider dropping her course. I decided to speak with her about what I was going through. This decision was my first step toward seeking the help that I so desperately needed. I went to her office hours prepared to start the conversation by discussing my academic work. Once seated in her office, I could not hold back my tears. She listened to me and she lifted me up. We talked for a while, and then she said that it was her lunchtime. I immediately prepared myself to leave, but she stopped me and asked if I would be able to join her for lunch. I accepted, and my life began to change.

During our lunch conversation, she told me a little about

her family and her educational background. I was amazed by how comfortable I felt with her. I told her a little about my family and my life goals. She suggested that I seek professional counseling to help with my depression. She told me that I was too intelligent and had too much potential to allow myself to continue to suffer. I followed her advice, and my journey toward peace of mind began. A busy college professor had paused and noticed my suffering. The light of God had showed up as her compassion, and it began to guide me out of the wilderness of loneliness and confusion. My professor was an attractive young white woman whose background was very different from mine. However, she seemed to understand my suffering, and she cared. She helped me to understand that the light of guidance and compassion can show up in any form or fashion. I remained in her class that semester and continued to learn valuable lessons related to my life and the study of psychology.

This wonderful, caring teacher followed up with me and gave me several referrals for therapists who could help. I sought professional help, and my life began to change for the better. It was not easy, but facing my fears was more than worth the effort it took.

I learned to view life from a different perspective. I began to read self-help books and inspirational materials related to my spiritual background. In addition, I studied psychology with great personal interest. My emotional childhood traumas were beginning to heal as I reflected upon past events with increased knowledge and greater emotional intelligence. I was gradually learning to let go of negative thinking.

I developed a love for the deep meanings I found in biblical scriptures, especially when they are spiritually interpreted. I spent countless hours studying everything that connected me with new ideas of trust, forgiveness, and compassion. I was on the path of releasing my mis-learnings and replacing them with positive, life-inspiring lessons. During these amazing years of spiritual renewal, I focused on one of the Hagar Church's most repeated quotations:

Wake up Ethiopians and see yourself coming into the glorious light of the sun. Prosperity is howling every day. Will you accept it? For, it will bring peace, joy, and happiness to your soul. Think for yourself and then you will create what you desire.

The more I focused on positive thinking, the less I felt the intensity of those childhood traumas. The relief I found in the practice of positive thinking sustains my faith even today that there is help in the light. Although I fall down, I get up and continue to seek the help that is always available.

Zorah's life journey also became a "light unto my path." She, despite her often untreated mental disorder, was a financial and emotional support for our family. She had friends who loved and supported her. Zorah's willingness to seek help also led to victories in her life. In fact, she became one of my guiding lights in overcoming whatever sadness, fear, or heartache I encountered. I began to reinterpret my wilderness experiences with Zorah. They became an example of how to survive emotional hardship by focusing on the solution rather than the problem. Zorah followed her light in the midst of a schizophrenic wilderness. The light led her to receive many years of happiness, and to do good works in our family and community.

During my adult life, Zorah and I shared many wonderful experiences. She demonstrated compassion for others, and I learned that from her. In my adulthood, I was able to return to her the compassion that she had given me so often. It took work and willingness on my part to reflect on the experiences that had caused me a great deal of anxiety and discomfort. I had to learn about forgiveness and search my heart and mind to truly be able to forgive Zorah and myself. Reading, studying, following spiritual principles, and seeking professional help when needed have led me to higher levels of understanding, forgiveness, and peace. Anyone who chooses to find relief from childhood trauma can find light in the wilderness by being willing to ask for and receive help.

The story of Hagar helps me to remember the magnificent power that comes from the act of seeking help. In the midst of the wilderness, she cried out for help, and the light of courage, wisdom, and understanding shone so brightly that she felt the presence of God. This ordinary person had an extraordinary experience. My own experiences of seeking and finding help in the wilderness have also been extraordinary. It is my humble prayer that all who are suffering from the residue of childhood trauma will find "Light in the Wilderness."

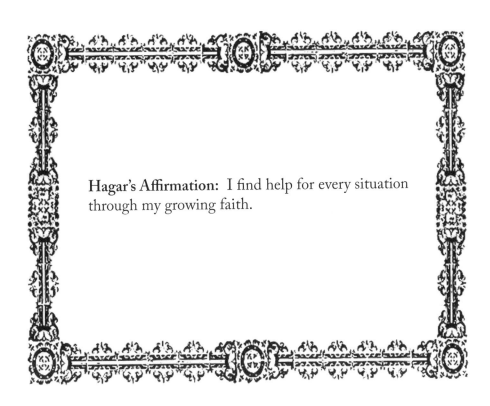

Hagar's Affirmation: I find help for every situation through my growing faith.

"Hate is too great a burden to bear. It injures the hater more than it injures the hated."

~Coretta Scott King~

LEARNING TO FORGIVE

I was running for my life, screaming for someone to help me. I knew that I would be tortured and killed if they caught me. Tears were streaming down my face, and my heart was pounding. The streets were so dark that I could not see where I was going, and I did not know where to find safety. An angry mob was chasing me, yelling words that vibrated with hostility. They hated me and wanted to kill me. Why?

Suddenly, I was awakened by my own screams. I sat up in bed, perspiring, and my heart was beating so fast that I could hardly breathe. As I struggled to gain composure, my mind became flooded with frightening thoughts. It was 1955, the dawn of the modern civil rights era. I was eleven years old and unaware that millions of people in America and around the world were about to suffer nightmares similar to mine. The night before that terrible dream, I had seen a picture of a fourteen year old boy named Emmett Till on television. He was laid out in a casket, and his face was so horribly disfigured that it terrified me. The newscaster said that Emmett's mother wanted an open casket so that the world could see what had been done to her son.

In the years that followed his murder, my youthful mind was assaulted by media images of black men hanging from trees in the South; women and men being beaten and dragged to jail for peacefully demonstrating for civil rights; and policemen turning water hoses and police dogs on children my age and younger. In time, Emmett Till's bludgeoned face might have faded from my memory. But the continuing reports of lynching and brutal attacks on colored people throughout the fifties and early sixties kept Emmett's face vividly stored in my memory. The nightmares I suffered were extensions of the terrible realities I witnessed almost daily.

I was always taught to obey authority figures. However, what was I to think when governors, mayors, and police chiefs announced on national television that they would die before allowing Negroes to integrate with whites? They did not want us in the classroom, at the lunch counter, on their jobs, or at their churches. It seemed to me that they just did not want us at all. I was young, but I had feelings. Being hated because of the color of my skin was hurtful, and it caused me to be fearful and cautious around white people. Even worse, it caused me to see myself, my skin color, hair texture, and facial features as a handicap, a negative. The image I saw in the mirror was the opposite of those labeled as beautiful in magazines and on the movie screens. If I don't look like them, and they are beautiful, then I must be ugly. The logic seemed sound to my young, impressionable mind. I felt like a stranger in a strange and hostile land.

I lived in the North, so I thought that perhaps I would be safe. "Just stay away from the South" became my planned strategy. It did not work. The racial violence came north. I learned later that it had always been there; I just didn't experience it first-hand until I was fifteen years old.

During the summer of 1959, my friends and I went on a picnic sponsored by a Philadelphia inner-city youth organization. We traveled by train to Forest Park, Pennsylvania, where a riot broke out shortly after we found a shady spot and began to relax. We were later told that the incident began with angry words between two young men: one black, and the other white. The fight escalated into a racially motivated attack on the visitors from the inner city. Hundreds of angry white people appeared armed with sticks, bats, and bricks. They were outraged by our presence and ready for blood. They beat every black boy and girl they could catch. Fortunately, I escaped harm, but one of my friends had to be admitted to the hospital and was kept several days before he was well enough to be discharged. As I stood in the middle of the chaos with no idea what was happening, I heard my girlfriend yelling my name. A young white man gestured to me to come to the small building where my friend and a crowd of other blacks were being sheltered. Park employees were trying to help us.

We waited nervously as ambulances and the state police arrived and began hurrying us into police vans and rushing us away. We were being rescued, but I knew that we were still in serious danger when I saw the large number of police officers lining the streets. We were taken to the railroad station, herded onto trains, and told to lie down on the floor. Angry white suburban boys and men crowded the station platform. They yelled threats and threw rocks and other objects as police tried to hold them off. I was nearly paralyzed with fear as I looked into the speechless faces of those who joined me on the floor of the train. Everyone seemed to be in shock, still not knowing what might happen. My mind suddenly shifted to my mother's wooden picnic basket; the gray sweater she had insisted I take in case it got chilly; and the only birthday gift my estranged father had ever given me – a used transistor radio that I treasured; all left behind. The train slowly pulled off and after a short while we were allowed to take our seats. Only a few whispering voices and occasional soft weeping was heard for the duration of the journey home.

That warm and sunny day in Forest Park, I learned the cold and dark reality that the same racial hatred that plagued the South also existed in the North. I became aware that there were places, sometimes within a mile or two of my home, that were not safe for people who looked like me. This personal encounter with the violence of racial hatred altered my reality and my behavior.

The following Monday morning I sat in the school auditorium for our regular assembly. As my classmates rose to recite the "Pledge of Allegiance," I stood silently with my hands at my sides. At the tender age of fifteen, I took my first political stand by refusing to say what I no longer believed: "With liberty and justice for all."

The Wilderness

I was angry. The more I learned about racism in America, past and present, the angrier I became. The chip that sat on my shoulder was invisible but could be felt by anyone in my presence; I felt it the most. I was prepared to counter anti-black comments, behaviors, and innuendos fast and furiously.

In the early 1960's I wondered if the white teachers and students at the recently desegregated high school I attended held inner thoughts similar to those expressed by Governor George Wallace and Alabama Commissioner of Public Safety, Eugene "Bull" Connor. Both of these men were highly publicized racists during the civil rights era. My thinking made most of my interracial interactions, in and outside of the black community, very uncomfortable. The bitterness I carried in my young heart caused me to be suspicious and judgmental toward all white people.

In an effort to protect myself from racial hatred and degradation, I wandered into the very wilderness that I sought to escape. The growing popularity and availability of television allowed me and countless numbers of black and white children to witness the barbarism that took place in middle twentieth-century America. Finding light in the wilderness of racial hatred would require that I learn the divine art of forgiveness.

The Light

Despite the seeming darkness of this wilderness experience, there was always some compassionate, morally ethical person who showed up to counter any belief in my mind that the senseless hatred and violence I witnessed was endorsed by everyone whose skin was different from mine.

I am grateful for the teachers, friends, and strangers who crossed my path, demonstrating again and again that ignorant behavior is not restricted to any particular skin color. Attending a racially mixed high school allowed me to get to know people of different races. I learned that, as Dr. Martin Luther King, Jr. stated, "people should be judged by the content of their character rather than the color of their skin." It is easy to lump people into groups and label them, but it is wise to use one's intellect and heart to measure each person for his or her value as a member of the human family.

I witnessed the bravery of people who gave their lives for social justice, and now I have lived long enough to be assured that we will all overcome some day. In 1963, four years after the Forest Park incident, my older sister Paulina and I marched with tens of thousands of people to the nation's capital for freedom and justice for all people. Just before completing this book, I returned to the Lincoln Memorial for the honor of celebrating the 50th anniversary of the famous March on Washington. Fifty years earlier, I had stood listening to the Rev. Dr. Martin Luther King, Jr. tell us of his dream. And in 2013, I stood and watched the first African American President of the United States of America, Barack Obama, revitalize the dream. His presence represented progress and proof that the dream can and will become fully manifest.

My biblical heroine Hagar was depicted as being different from Abraham and his people. She was used sexually for procreation, and while pregnant, she was abused by her mistress.

Hagar fled into the wilderness feeling the sting of being delegated as "the other" and "less than." It was by faith that she returned to her mistress, trusting in God's promise to bless her offspring.

Hagar must have learned to forgive, because when Abraham died, her beloved son Ishmael and his brother Isaac went together to bury their father. Even after being harshly mistreated, Hagar found it in her heart to raise a son who supported the family that had once abandoned them.

Every generation has an opportunity to move civilization forward and solve the problem of human injustice by using the most powerful force on earth, divine LOVE! The magnificent power of love is born out of the deep human capacity to forgive.

I practice forgiveness on a daily basis as an act of self-love. It releases me from the toxic poison of hatred and bitterness and awakens me into the divine light of wisdom and understanding. It is my prayer that the world will be embraced by the light of forgiveness. Please love yourself enough today to forgive someone.

Hagar's Affirmation: I release resentment and blame, replenishing my soul with peace and gratitude.

"Someone was hurt before you, wronged before you, hungry before you, frightened before you, beaten before you, humiliated before you, raped before you... yet, someone survived...You can do anything you choose to do."

~Maya Angelou~

CHOOSING TO HEAL

By my mid-forties, I had reached a point in my life and career that surpassed my own expectations. My personal and spiritual growth was evidenced by the supportive and loving relationships I enjoyed. I was academically credentialed and held a position of status in an elite institution of higher education. The emotional struggles that had once plagued my daily life were now infrequent and subdued. However, the residue of past wilderness experiences were ready for a deeper healing.

My phone rang, and it was my secretary announcing that my three o'clock appointment had arrived. I opened the office door and invited the young man to enter and have a seat. I had granted this young research student an interview to help with his academic project. He was writing about the effects of Peace Corps service on the lives of former volunteers. He had found my name in public documents, listed among volunteers who had served within the first ten years of the establishment of the United States Peace Corps (1961-1971).

Formalities completed, the interviewer asked permission to record the session. I agreed. He had asked most of his questions, and I was enjoying reminiscing about my time in the Peace Corps and the educational and professional successes since leaving my host country in Central West Africa. Then he asked an unexpected question that completely shifted my relaxed, professional composure. He asked, "Did you encounter any abuse or violence while serving overseas?" I sat silently for a few seconds as the memory of my buried secret streamed through my mind. My heart began to beat like a loud drum that could be heard for miles. The blood raced through my veins, feeling cold and toxic as my throat began to tighten. I was shocked at these physical responses to a question that I had avoided for twenty years. I had contrived a story to explain my early return from the Peace Corps and repeated it so often that I nearly believed it to be true. The interviewer's question had caused a knot of anxiety to form in the pit of my stomach.

I heard a voice in my head screaming, "Just say no! Just say no!" But there was a soft, yet stronger voice coming from my soul that said, "Tell the truth." I decided to follow my soul. It had yearned for freedom from this malignant secret for many years. Before I uttered a word, I relived the entire horrific scene in my mind.

When I first arrived in Africa, I was twenty-four years old, excited, and wide-eyed. It seemed unimaginable that a poor little black girl from North Philly was standing on African soil. I was overcome by the magnificent homeland of my ancestors and felt that I was the long lost daughter of a land that had never forgotten me. I felt at home!

Within a few days of getting settled, I was called into the medical office for a general health follow-up. The Peace Corps nurse reviewed my health record and asked whether I'd had any issues since leaving basic training. I explained that I had noticed small, wart-like growths around my pelvic area. The nurse examined the area and told me that the growths appeared to be a common problem that occurred due to extreme heat. She gave me instructions to help the problem but said that I should follow up with the new doctor when he arrived in two weeks.

When the doctor arrived, I had to wait another few weeks for him to get situated before he was settled in and able to see patients. When I finally saw the doctor, the problem had gotten worse, and I was worried. He examined me and said that he would need to do a pelvic exam and take a pap smear. I never liked internal exams, but if it had to be done, so be it. When the exam ended, the doctor told me that he would need to order a medication to burn off the warts. But the good news was, the warts were only on the outside of my pelvic area. I had to wait another few weeks for the medication to arrive at the clinic.

The treatment process was excruciating. The only way to tell that a wart had been entirely removed was when the chemical began to burn my skin in this very sensitive area. Several weeks later, the doctor made an appointment for me to come into his office on a Saturday to see if the scars were healing appropriately. I was on the examination table with my feet in the stirrups as the doctor told me that the wounds had cleared up nicely and I would not need any further treatments. I was so happy that this terrible ordeal had come to an end! Or so I thought. What happened next was a nightmare that changed my life and left me stunned and humiliated.

My doctor, who had previously always behaved in a professional manner, was on now top of me. He did not speak as he pushed his body against mine, pinning my body down with his own. He grabbed my arms as I struggled in disbelief at what was happening to me. I remember telling him to get off me, yelling for him to stop, but he acted as if he did not hear me. Nobody could hear me because we were alone in his closed office. He entered me, and I fought helplessly against his strength as he ignored my frantic pleas. The next thing I remember was him standing in front of me, telling me to get up and put on my panties, which were neatly folded on a chair. His voice was cold and stern, and I silently followed his orders.

I stood in his office speechless, questioning whether this was real. He appeared calm and told me that he was going to take me home. We stepped outside of the small clinic, and he went to the side of the car and opened the passenger door. I robotically climbed into the seat as if in a dream.

My house was only a short distance from the office where I worked as a secretary, and his medical office was in the rear of that building. He had a bag of red apples in the Jeep, and he took one out and placed it in my hands, which were folded on my lap. I remained silent, as if my voice had been muted. I stared down at the red apple in my hand; my hand felt disconnected from my body.

The Jeep pulled up in front of my courtyard, and I climbed out of the car and walked silently toward my door. I could hear the doctor saying something, but his words were like a distant echo that could not penetrate the thick fog that surrounded me. I entered my house and sat down in the first chair I reached. After an undetermined amount of time, I realized that I had been just staring at the red apple that was still in my hand. I sat the apple on the side table near my chair and stood up. I had decided that all I wanted to do was take a shower. I wanted to be clean. I grabbed my washcloth and towel and made my way to the shower. Although the water was cold, I wanted that shower to never end....

I suddenly became aware that the interviewer was sitting patiently, awaiting my response. I felt like I had traveled ten thousand miles to revisit this horrific event. The vividness of the memory sprang to life as if it had occurred a moment ago. I told the young man that while I was in my host country, I had been raped by the Peace Corps doctor. I was shocked by my own admission of what had happened. Up until that moment, I had only shared that secret with my best friend, who had been date raped while in college. I expected the interviewer to be shocked as well. He was not. He told me that he had heard many stories of rape and assault of volunteers while serving overseas. He wrote in his notes as I asked to be reassured that my name would not be mentioned in his book.

We completed the interview with a few less provocative

questions and answers before ending the session. I sat in my office after the young man left, knowing that it was time to do more therapy and a great deal more spiritual work. The most enduring and damaging part of this traumatic life event was still to be uncovered.

My emotional and immature strategy for dealing with the assault was to try to forget that it had happened. This strategy abruptly failed when my extremely regular menstrual cycle did not appear. Panic erupted inside every inch of my body as I realized that I was pregnant. How could this be happening to me? Wasn't being raped enough? What was I to do? I was 10,000 miles away from family, friends, and my boyfriend! All I could think of was that I wanted my period to come on. These words repeated themselves in my head over and over again like a mantra. I decided to go to the only person that I thought could help restore my menstrual cycle—the person who had caused the problem. In my distraught, desperate, and angry state of mind, I sought the assistance of my rapist. I did not want to be pregnant; I did not even want to think about it or consider any options. I wanted my monthly menstrual cycle to resume, period! The next day at work, I walked to the rear of my office building into the doctor's office. I stood in the room where I had been raped nearly six weeks earlier, looking into the face of my rapist. Without ceremony, I bluntly told him that I had not gotten my period and that I wanted him to make it come on. He said that I was just imagining things. He told me that my body was probably just adjusting to the change in environment. He also asked me if I had been sexually involved with anyone. My head almost exploded! I told him that my condition was because of what he had done to me. He said that I was being silly, and he refused to do anything. I left his office in a rage and slammed the door behind me. In a fit of desperation, I went directly to the front office of the Peace Corps site director, Larry, and told him everything. I was fortunate that he listened and responded in a supportive manner. He asked me if I was willing to go with him and his wife, the Peace Corps nurse, to take a pregnancy test. I agreed, and weeks later he gave me the news that I had intuitively known all along. I was pregnant. Larry told me that an investigation was being made into the situation and that he had spoken to the doctor. He told me that I would be sent to a hospital in Frankford, Germany for medical treatment. However, before I was to leave, an incident at the United States government facility in Germany caused my travel arrangements to be changed, and I was sent back to the United States for medical and psychological treatment.

I arrived in Washington, D.C. in January of 1969. By my request, my family was never informed. Accommodations at a downtown hotel were provided for me, and I was given a small stipend for meals and cab fares to the medical appointments that had been made for me. They included several psychiatrists. The entire experience was quite surreal. I felt disconnected from everything, including my own body. I wanted my life back to what it had been, and nothing else seemed to matter. I was full of self-pity, shame, and self-blame. My mental distress kept my mind wandering in and out of reality. I wanted this nightmare to end, and I was willing to do whatever was needed to make it happen.

The medical experts who worked for the government determined that I was not mentally stable enough to endure the pregnancy. I was approved for what they called a "therapeutic abortion." I spent two weeks in a rather exclusive mental health facility prior to the procedure. While recovering, I received a call from the State Department asking me to contact my mother. When I called, she told me that she had received my belongings in a trunk from the Peace Corps office in Africa. She had been frantically calling government offices trying to find out where I was and what had happened to me. They didn't give her any information, but they told her that they would contact me and ask me to call home. I told my mother that I had become ill and was sent back to the states for treatment, and that I was perfectly well now. She sent a local relative to the hospital to see about me, and fortunately, my story was never questioned.

After leaving the hospital, I stayed with my relative for a week or so while trying to decide whether to return to my post in Africa or end my Peace Corps service and return home. I could find no joy in the idea of returning overseas. I wanted to be in familiar surroundings with my family and friends. I was healing physically and anxious to return home to what I thought would be a normal life. My emotional wounds remained inside, untreated and destined to fester and grow into decades of wilderness.

The Wilderness

Being raped lasted a few moments, but the emotional trauma remained with me for decades. I was unwilling to admit what had happened. It was too painful to face and too easy to deny. The story of why I came home after only six short months of Peace Corps service was simple and plausible; without the painful details, it was actually true. The story I told was that I had become ill and was sent back to the States for medical treatment. After recuperating at home, I had decided not to return to Peace Corps service and was discharged due to my medical circumstances. That was my story, and I stuck to it. I stuck to it for so long that I nearly forgot the dreadful details I had buried inside. The details, however, remained alive and exposed themselves in unexpected and uninvited moments of my life.

Sudden or unexpected touching was difficult for me to tolerate. My body would stiffen, or I would withdraw abruptly from innocent attempts by friends and loved ones to hug me. My physical reaction to being touched caused many awkward and uncomfortable moments in my relationships and social interactions. I avoided sex with my boyfriend for many months by claiming to still be healing from a surgery to remove internal warts from my vagina. I think the image itself was enough to discourage him. Eventually, I was comfortable enough to be intimate with the man that I thought I would marry, have children with, and live happily ever after. Our relationship lasted two chaotic years after my return from the Peace Corps, but eventually I became convinced that he could not be trusted. (I would later learn that my mistrust was justified.) Breaking up with him intensified my chronic state of depression and alternating state of hyper anxiety. In the years that followed, I engaged in a number of behaviors indicative of a severe wilderness experience: five failed relationships, a short-lived marriage, two suicide attempts, marijuana abuse, episodes of promiscuity, and a progressive food addiction. These complications did not stop me from presenting an "I'm okay" public persona.

During these inner wilderness years, I avoided ever having a gynecological examination. I self-medicated any female problems I encountered until they became too severe to manage. I hemorrhaged during my menstrual cycles for at least six months, while avoiding my medical doctor's advice to see a gynecologist. I always had an excuse or would conveniently forget my appointments. Finally, I went to Planned Parenthood, where I thought I would be safe and could easily be treated by a female doctor. My visit determined that I had massive fibroid tumors that would require surgery. The surgery resulted in a full hysterectomy that rendered me unable to give birth. By that time, I had already determined that I was emotionally unable to be the mother that I had dreamt of being. Somehow, this loss of the potentiality of giving life led me to thinking about the possibility of recovering my own life. I cried out in the wilderness of despair for help. I asked for light, and it came.

The Light

One of the positive things about this trauma is that it numbed me, allowing my life to continue, albeit in a robotic state. Many years passed before I could find the light in this wilderness experience. However, as I went deeper into self-reflection, I found an inner urging to heal. I wanted to reach a level of healing that would enable me to speak my truth so that others who had been violated would know that they were not alone.

Encouraged by one of my spiritual teachers, I sought additional therapeutic help that could now tie into my spiritual growth and understanding. I was finally returning to my early spiritual teachings that I had ignored for far too long. My faith was, as scripture says, "as tiny as a mustard seed," but it was enough to light my path through the process of soul healing.

I prayed a lot. I read and studied books that were designed to promote emotional healing. Eventually, I was able to forgive the doctor who raped me; and more importantly, I was able to forgive myself for the hurt and harm I had caused myself. I forgave myself for the blame, guilt, and shame I had carried within for so long.

My secret was unveiled, and I could see the light in that long past wilderness experience. For many years after that interview, I have shared this story with others who have been violated in some devastating manner. It has helped us all to heal and to understand that we do not have to define ourselves by what happens to us. Rather, we define ourselves by how we deal with the circumstances that life serves us.

I choose to tell my story because 4,000 years before me, a young black woman named Hagar--pregnant, abused, and alone—cried out in the wilderness and was guided by the light. I choose to tell my story because a modern day mother of wisdom, Maya Angelou, reminded all of us that "We can choose to do anything we want to do." My burdens are fewer and my journey is brighter because I choose to heal on a daily basis. What do you choose: wilderness or light?

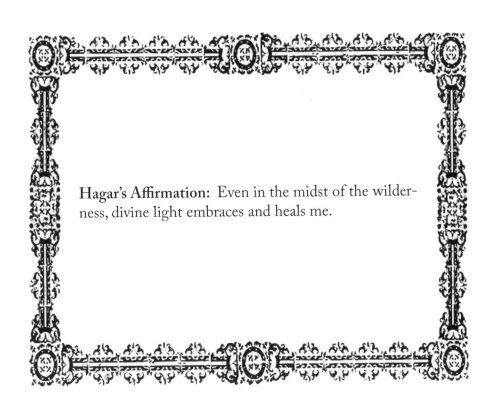

Hagar's Affirmation: Even in the midst of the wilderness, divine light embraces and heals me.

"Don't wait around for other people to be happy for you. Any happiness you get you've got to make yourself."

~Alice Walker~

I had been crying for hours, and it was late into the night. Finally, the tears stopped, and I was numb. My body felt heavy, but my emotional numbness was pleasant; I appreciated the lack of feeling. I slowly climbed the stairs of my mother's house, where I was visiting for the weekend. Her bedroom door was ajar, and I entered carefully to avoid waking her. Fully clothed, I climbed into bed next to her. My heart was broken. The love of my life had betrayed me, and my eyes had been opened to eight long years of lies and deceptions. I felt that I would never be able to love or trust again. This betrayal unleashed every pain, disappointment, fear, and loss I had ever experienced in my short twenty-seven years.

As I lay still next to my mother, tears began to roll down my face again. I was surprised that my body could produce more tears. "There must be an endless ocean inside of me," I thought. I held my breath and tried to muffle the sound of the sobbing that was pushing to escape my body. This was personal; it was not something that I discussed with others, especially not my mother. Our relationship was loving and proper, but not intimate. I heard my mother gently say without moving a muscle, "What's the matter?" I, too, lay absolutely still, and slowly forcing my words through the quiet tears I answered, "Mom, I'm so unhappy." She calmly responded, "Baby, you'll find happiness again." Both of us laid in the stillness of the approaching dawn, communicating silently, heart to heart as we had never done before. We drifted off to sleep and never spoke another word about that moment. I believe that my mother's quiet and assuring words came from a deep understanding of the emotional pain I was experiencing. She did not need to know the facts; she knew her child was hurting. She must have experienced this unbearable pain at some dark moment in her own life. Her empathy suggested that she knew this pain intimately. She must have known that I was in no way ready or able to describe or discuss my intense feelings. There was too much that I needed to learn and understand about myself. I was grateful for her few encouraging words. Her response was exactly what I needed, a quiet loving soul to be with me in that moment; a warm, breathing body ensuring me that I was alive and that I would, one day, be able to live and love again. The sharp and immediate pain of discovering my boyfriend's betrayal was a traumatic event in my life. I gained some degree of relief by listening to him beg for my forgiveness. I would meet with him in the weeks that followed my earth-shaking discovery of his years of infidelity. I was embarrassed that I had been so naïve for so many years. I could not believe his words, and it would be a long time, in and out of relationship wilderness, before I could trust myself to love again.

Cora Lee Ferguson Darrah (author's mother)
1903-1985

The Wilderness

My heart was broken, and I did not know how to fix it. My state of mind fit every aspect of wilderness: confusion, loneliness, and despair. My first instinct was to protect myself from ever having to feel so miserable again. I went from blaming myself for being stupid enough to trust, to blaming him for being a lying, callous cheat. I felt absent from my body and my confusion was almost debilitating.

I went through a period of not eating or sleeping to over-eating and over-sleeping. While in my state of mental wilderness, I listened to his excuses, but nothing he said penetrated the wall of hurt that his betrayal had so quickly built. I was angry. I had given him what I thought was the best of me. If I could not trust the person I had given my heart, then I obviously was not capable of judging the character of anyone. This was the thinking that would lead me into chronic episodes of suffering in the wilderness.

I was no longer an innocent romantic; I was, so I thought, a mature woman who had experienced the reality of "love" relationships. I would not be fooled again. When confronted with discontentment in a relationship, I would demand that the situation be corrected, or I would leave.

When future opportunities for romantic relationships arrived, my goal was to be safe. I was aware that someone could look into my eyes with the appearance of sincerity and lie without blinking. This wilderness experience was the most resistant to the light because of my closed heart.

I showed no mercy to the men I dated. Looking back, I wonder why so many men seemed attracted to me. Perhaps I was attracting men who felt that they deserved distrust and mistreatment. The men I dated came and went before any level of intimacy developed. My standards were high, and my rules were strict. Tardiness, broken dates, criticisms, or any slight missteps on their part were grounds for termination. I saw many bewildered faces as I informed them that it was over. I was safe, but I was also lonely, hurt, and bitter. I was avoiding hurt feelings, but I was also avoiding feeling loved. Genuinely expressing love to another person was exciting and fulfilling, but I was depriving myself of that experience. Unhappy and lonely, my superficial relationships reminded me of my inability to trust or accept affection. Life had become a burden, and I knew intuitively that I did not want to spend the rest of my life in this manner. I called this my "Hard-hearted Hannah" period of wilderness. It was time for a change. I prayed for relief from the coldness that surrounded my heart. My prayers in the wilderness brought light into my life.

The Light

It was the end of May and the college semester was almost over. One of my classmates, Jason, invited several of us to a college scholarship benefit dance. My friend Rhonda and I bought tickets and went to the event together. Jason introduced us to one of the coordinators of the event. Tony was a handsome, polite young community activist who appeared to be very dedicated to helping minorities receive educational support. He and I seemed to be immediately attracted to one another. Our eyes locked into a deep and sensual stare. I felt a sense of romance in my heart for the first time in more than a year. Tony thanked us for attending and gently shook my hand again before excusing himself to return to his duties. He was one of the designated speakers, and when he took the stage he had my full attention.

Tony's remarks were thoughtful and passionate as he encouraged us to donate generously to the scholarship fund. I was deeply touched by his message and his obvious intellect and compassion for others. The audience gave him an enthusiastic applause as he exited the stage. I was more than impressed and hopeful that I would get to spend some time with him during the dance. Unfortunately, the event was coming to an end, and I had not seen him. Rhonda and I were making our way to the door when suddenly, Tony appeared and touched my arm. He apologized for not having had the time to talk with me during the party. He explained that the business part of the event obligated him to attend a meeting after the party as well. He told me that he wanted very much to talk with me. He asked if he could have my phone number. Without my usual hesitation or sarcasm, I gave him my phone number.

Several weeks passed, and I did not receive a call from Tony. I wondered if I had mistakenly given him the wrong number. My feelings went back and forth from dismissing him as another ego-centered guy trying to up his quota of female phone numbers, to thinking that there might be a legitimate reason that kept him from calling. The fact that I was undecided indicated that my heart was beginning to open. I was determined not to allow my past hurts to cause me to prejudge all men as potential betrayers. Tony would have been a perfect test case for my ability to open my heart again, if he had called as I expected. I decided to put him out of my mind and try to enjoy my summer vacation.

I had registered for a course during the second summer session, and it happened that Jason had signed up for the same class. We greeted each other and talked briefly about how the summer was going. I asked him if he had seen his friend Tony recently. He said that he had not, but that the last time he saw him, Tony asked about me. I said, "Oh really? Well, when you see him again, please tell him that if he's not going to use my phone number, he should dispose of it." I was rather proud of the suave manner in which I delivered my comment. I was not usually that clever or fluent with matters of an emotional nature. Jason said that he would deliver the message the next time he ran into Tony. Evidently, they were not close friends because Jason mentioned that he only saw Tony at meetings and events sponsored by their organization.

The summer went swiftly, and it was time for me to return to school. I attended a college that was approximately fifty miles from my home, and my planned ride had just cancelled. I was making phone calls trying to get a last minute ride when the phone rang, and it was Tony. He asked how I was doing, and I told him that I was in the middle of trying to get a ride back to school and could not talk with him at the moment. He asked if he could drive me. I probably would have said no, but I was desperate to get back to school in time for my first class early the following morning. Tony seemed excited about my affirmative response and said that he would pick me up in thirty minutes. I gave him my address, and exactly thirty minutes later Tony was at my doorstep looking more handsome than I had remembered. Nonetheless, I was determined not to allow myself to be seduced by his charm. His long absence needed to be explained.

I politely introduced Tony to my family and his relaxed, personable manner reminded me why I had been so infatuated with him when we first met. Without prompting, Tony respectfully assured my mother that he would deliver me safely to school. He picked up my suitcase and gave me time to say my goodbyes. He opened the car and waited until I had adjusted myself into the seat. He closed the door, quickly put the suitcase in his trunk, and was sitting beside me, seemingly all in one smooth motion. This man was amazing! My heart was pounding as I silently commanded my emotions to settle down. He asked me where we were going, and I realized that he had not asked earlier. I told him where I was going and then asked what he would have done if I had said Boston University! He laughed and said, "Then we would be on our way to Boston." I was speechless. We started on a journey that would profoundly and delightfully change my life.

Tony's car radio softly supplied smooth jazz music that provided a perfect background for conversation. "When I arrived at your house tonight, I realized that I had been there before," Tony said. I looked at him, waiting for the punch line of what must be another bit of humor. Tony's face, however, was dead serious. "Once I entered your house, I was absolutely sure that it was the same place that Bobby Jones had brought me nearly thirteen years ago." I looked at Tony in shock as he went on to describe that late summer afternoon when I was barely sixteen years old. It felt surreal, and yet my memory was kicking in, and I was beginning to recall that day. "Yes," I said. "I remember my friend Bobby stopping by with a guest. I called my girlfriend Cathy, who lived three houses away, to come over to play monopoly with us." Tony replied, "Yes, I remember that Cathy was a tall, thin girl who wore eyeglasses." I excitedly replied, "You're right! We're still friends." My head was spinning, trying to put everything that was happening into perspective. This amazingly handsome, smart man who seemed to be very attracted to me had been in my presence years earlier. We had talked, played a board game, and eaten snacks together. An unbelievable sense of magic filled the air. Tony and I were both excited about what was turning into a "meant to be" meeting of our souls.

It was beginning to turn dark on this pleasant late summer evening, and the feeling was so euphoric that I hoped it would never end. However, there was still the matter of what took him so long to contact me. Despite all of the positive energy, my heart was still too bruised to accept the joy I was experiencing. My mind jumped back to the thought of why Tony had waited the entire summer before calling me. I was hesitant to bring up the matter for fear that his explanation would jeopardize this enchanted evening.

We were approximately twenty minutes from school when Tony said, "I want to tell you why I waited so long to contact you. When we met three months ago, I was in the process of ending a two year relationship that had not been working for some time. I needed to make sure that it was completely settled, and that nothing and no one would stand in the way of getting to know you better. I've been hurt before," he continued, "and I only treat others with the respect, openness, and honesty that I expect from them." This was music to my ears because his explanation made sense to me, and that was exactly what I needed. My journey to open my heart again was off to a great start.

Tony and I spent as much time together as our busy academic schedules would allow. We went out to eat, took in an occasional movie, and spent many Saturday afternoons in the library. Both of us loved live theater, so he planned wonderful weekends in New York where we enjoyed off-Broadway performances and the excitement of the big city. Life was good, and I was mending my heart through the love, compassion, and caring that Tony showed me. I believe that he was the light that was sent in response to my cry for help in the wilderness.

I learned, slowly but surely, to trust again. Tony gave me the opportunity to build my self-confidence and to recognize my value as an intelligent, talented, and powerful woman. He always complimented me for my achievements and encouraged me to grow emotionally, mentally, and spiritually. I confided in Tony, and he never judged me. We became more than lovers: we were friends.

Tony and I graduated two years after we met, and we both received fellowships to attend universities that were quite a distance apart. We knew that our lives were about to take us down different paths. Separating from Tony was an emotionally difficult task for me.

My first year in graduate school was extremely challenging, and I cried regularly, but not alone. Tony was always on the other end of the phone, listening, comforting, and encouraging me to claim my own happiness. Tony supported me emotionally until I was able to stand strongly on my own. It is incredible how the divine universal force brought forth exactly what I needed for as long as I needed it. I remain eternally grateful. It is never too late to open your heart again. The light that guided my path to an open heart came in the form of an honest, faithful man.

I believe that Hagar, the Egyptian slave girl turned matriarch, had opened her heart again by returning to the camp of Abraham and Sarah to give birth to Abraham's seed. Years later, she was put out of her home and sent to make her own way with her child. Hagar's extraordinary experience of seeing the light of God in the wilderness carried her through multiple wilderness experiences. She, through her son Ishmael, gained a rich and vast kingdom as God had promised. Hagar opened her heart, allowing Ishmael to be reunited with his brother Isaac. Such bonds are not possible without the presence of an open heart. I give thanks for the gift of having my heart opened again and the happiness that it brings into my life.

Hagar's Affirmation: My heart is open and receptive to give and receive abundant divine love.

"Your willingness to look at your darkness is what empowers you to change."

~Iyanla Vanzant~

SPEAKING MY TRUTH

My sister Lisa was about fifty-three years old and had suffered from chronic depression for many years. I received a phone call from her one afternoon while at work. She politely asked how I was doing. I replied that I was doing quite well. Lisa had never called me while I was at work, so I wondered what was on her mind. She casually told me that she was calling to say goodbye. I asked her where she was going, to which she responded meekly, "Well, I'm not sure, but I want you to know that I love you." I replied, "I love you too, Lisa."

My intuition and professional training in counseling prompted me to calmly ask Lisa if she was planning to hurt herself. She quietly answered that she just wanted to be out of pain. Nervousness formed in the pit of my stomach. I knew that Lisa was serious. I asked her if she had taken pills; she said no. I asked in a nonchalant tone that even surprised me, "How are you planning to do it?" She told me that she had a knife, and that after she finished serving her companion Clarence his breakfast, she was going to clean up the dishes, go upstairs, and cut her wrists. Lisa and I were having this surreal conversation with eerie composure. I told Lisa that I loved her very much and that I would be very sad if she harmed herself. I faked an interruption and told Lisa that I would call her back in a moment due to a work matter, and she agreed. Whenever Lisa was depressed, she would say that she wished she was dead or had never been born. Most of our immediate family members were used to hearing these types of comments from her. I knew in my soul that this time was different. I could hear the realness of finality in Lisa's voice. My past, still undisclosed, suicide attempts connected me with the lifeless yet resolute tone in her voice. I hung up the phone and immediately called 911 to report my sister's intentions. I gave the dispatch operator Lisa's name and address, and my phone number. The operator kept me on the line until a patrol car was in the vicinity and heading toward her home.

I told the operator that I needed to call my sister back, and he asked that I not tell her that they were coming. I agreed, hung up the phone, and redialed Lisa. Clarence answered the phone:

"Hello, Clarence, is Lisa in the room with you?" "Yes," he replied. "Please just listen and don't let her know it's me on the phone." Clarence was completely shocked when I told him that Lisa was planning to harm herself and that the police were on the way to their house. I asked him to remain calm, and he again quietly agreed. He then said, "I think they're here."

I could hear the police officer as he entered the house. I heard what sounded like a very well trained and experienced officer ask, "Are you Lisa?" "Yes," she politely responded. When he asked whether she had a knife in her possession, she again responded, "Yes." He asked her where it was, and she told him that it was in the pocket of the bathrobe she was wearing. "Can I take it from your pocket?" he asked, without missing a beat. Lisa gave her consent. I learned later that it was a sharp-bladed butcher knife that could have accomplished exactly what she intended.

I sat at my desk completely still and barely breathing, listening as the officer told Lisa that he wanted to take her to a hospital to make sure that she was not injured. Again, Lisa complied. Clarence said he would go with her, and I told him that I was on my way as well. I hung up the phone, took a deep breath, and then sobbed like a baby. I had to travel about thirty miles out of town to meet them at their local hospital. A one-hour drive in mid-morning traffic seemed like an eternity. In the privacy of my car I cried aloud at the thought of losing my sister. My anguish deepened as I realized the degree of pain and suffering my loved ones would have endured had my own suicide attempts not failed. I was filled with remorse and gratitude at the same time. I prayed, cried, and prayed again for the rest of my journey. Lisa was admitted into the hospital and treated for severe chronic depression. The doctors wanted to administer electric shock treatment during her hospital stay. Lisa adamantly refused. I was then and am now completely supportive of a person's right for autonomy in regard to his or her own medical treatment. Lisa knew what she wanted, and she was able to manage her condition with medication.

Although she never expressed it verbally, I believe that Lisa felt my compassion and my respect for her. She trusted me more than she trusted most people, and when she passed away at the mature age of eighty, I was left to handle her final arrangements. Lisa knew that I would do everything in my power to honor her final requests.

Lisa was a caring person whose life journey was filled with wilderness experiences, yet she gave light to so many others. She carried the burdens of others as if they were her own. Despite her battle with chronic and severe depression, when she could, she would do anything to help her relatives and friends. I believe that Lisa's concern for others may have overshadowed her own self-care. She valued and showed compassion for others but for much of her life was unable to give these life-sustaining gifts to herself. This behavior is not uncommon among women who must fight daily to be recognized as human beings, worthy of equal human rights. Self-sacrifice in exchange for survival has been a part of womanhood for millenniums. This is why, I suspect, Hagar cried out in the wilderness and it is why so many of us, her modern day sisters, still suffer in the wilderness.

The Wilderness

I felt guilty because I had kept my own suicide attempts a secret from everyone, including Lisa. I wondered whether she would have been able to avoid going down that same road if I had shared my experience with her earlier. I thought to myself, What if Lisa's suicide attempt had turned out differently? I shudder to think of the guilt I would have felt. My mind went back to a time that I was in the same place of despair as Lisa was on that fateful day.

While in college I had suffered some of my most severe wilderness experiences. I was an academic overachiever and a social underachiever. At 27 years old, I was a nontraditional student with a lot to prove. I was stressed out, sleep-deprived, and recently diagnosed as chronic depressive. My boyfriend had grown weary of my mood swings, as he accurately defined them. He phoned me one day and said that he had reunited with his former girlfriend and that our relationship was over. She was sitting with him as he made the call. I was devastated by his rejection and embarrassed by the manner in which he chose to do it. I felt betrayed, angry, and powerless to do anything about it. (Anything legal, at least!) Worst of all, I was completely incapable of focusing on studying and writing final papers. A sense of desperation consumed my entire being. I chose wine and marijuana over the next several days as an escape from what felt like unbearable pain. I sat alone in my apartment in a drug-induced state and considered suicide. I wanted to escape the pain of rejection, responsibility, and disappointment. I wanted out, and overdosing on prescription drugs seemed like a convenient way to exit.

Two earlier suicide gestures were not like this one. I think that those were more of a dramatic expression of my pain. Earlier attempts to harm myself were impulsive actions to demonstrate my despair. I used methods that were more stupid than fatal and made sure that the person I blamed for my sorrow was present. This time I was looking forward to being free from a pain that felt deep-rooted and unrelenting. I sat alone, thinking of every painful, hurtful, and embarrassing thing that had ever happened to me. It was the grandest pity party imaginable. When I had thoroughly convinced myself that it was time for my life to end, I took a bottle of pills. I laid down fully clothed, awaiting my death. I was found semiconscious by friends and rushed to the hospital. What caused my admission to the psychiatric unit of the hospital was kept a secret from my family. The storyline was: "I was under too much pressure from school, got sick, went to the hospital, got treated, and now I'm back to normal." An important lesson was gained from this last suicide attempt. It came to me almost as a revelation: Our lives do not belong to us alone. Life is a sacred gift given to us by a higher power and must be ended only through the source that gave it. Unfortunately, I had not advanced enough into the light to see how speaking my truth could benefit me and be a source of healing for others. I had not shared this precious lesson of personal self-disclosure with Lisa. If I had, her nearly tragic moment might have been avoided. My story might have encouraged her to seek professional assistance and know that she was not alone. As my mind came back to the present, I prayed that Lisa would be alright and that I would be given the opportunity, at an appropriate time, to share my story with her.

The Light

The lesson that I learned from my experience with Lisa and by reflecting on my own wilderness stories was to value the healing power of sincere and intentional self-disclosure. It created an enduring bond between us. My self-disclosures have allowed me to take a deeper look into the darkness of my wilderness experiences. By looking at my past from a different vantage point, I have been able to see my situations more clearly. I decided to grow my faith through the process of self-reflection and self-disclosure as I prayed for enlightenment. I believe today, without a doubt, that "Faith, even the size of a tiny mustard seed, can move mountains" (Matthew 17:20). When I asked for help and remained open and receptive to receiving it, my faith attracted into my life that which I needed.

My motivation for sharing the suffering that I have experienced is to let others know how I came through those most difficult times. Perhaps because I have shared these adversities, someone will be encouraged to face the darkness of their wilderness experience and find the light that can heal their suffering.

Lisa survived her planned suicide attempt and lived to have many happy and fulfilling years. I was so grateful that she came to a point that led her to face her mental health challenges and choose life. It was a heart-filling experience to witness Lisa as she reclaimed her life.

Our entire family supported and loved her back to a healthy state of being. This event brought all of us closer together. There were fewer secrets in our family after that, and because Lisa was willing to do the work needed for her recovery, my whole family was able to witness and grow from the divine healing light that abides in the darkness of the wilderness. That light is within us all.

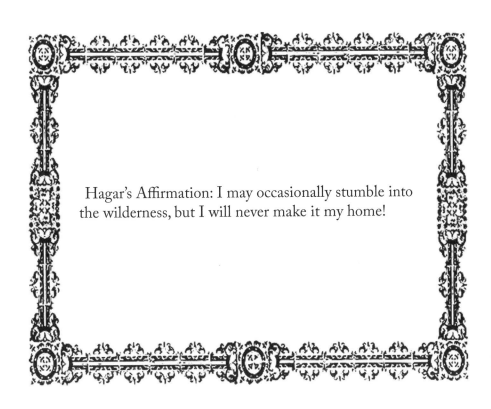

Hagar's Affirmation: I may occasionally stumble into the wilderness, but I will never make it my home!

"…No matter what our age or condition, there are still untapped possibilities within us and new beauty waiting to be born."

~Helen Keller~

LOVING MYSELF

I had fallen asleep in a chair while bingeing on chocolate candy and watching late night television. I woke up choking so violently that I became really afraid that I would not be able to halt the closing of my throat. A piece of chocolate had lodged there. I felt like I was about to die as I raised my arms above my head to try to open my airway.

When I regained my composure, I looked to my side and saw the bags of junk food that I had been eating that night. I reached down and got a handful of potato chips, then returned to my routine of eating and watching television until I was unconscious enough to fall asleep again. I was living my life in the wilderness of food addiction every night.

During the day, I played the role of a normal person. I worked and interacted with others quite well. People did not know how sad and confused I was, and I did everything in my power to keep them from finding out. By the time my workday ended, I was exhausted. I stayed up late every night eating processed junk food, and during the day I compulsively thought about what I would eat that night.

It was emotionally draining to be obsessed with food. I was confronted by food all day in the workplace. I would restrain myself from overeating in front of people. But, if I could hide the food or pretend that I was going to give it to someone else, I would. My life was no different than that of a crack addict. My drug of choice was plentiful, and people would give it away regularly. In fact, many people would insist that I have something to eat and be upset if I refused. There was no need for me to roam the streets like my sisters and brothers whose drug of choice was illegal and expensive. I have no doubt that I would have sold my body if food had the restrictions and was dispensed like cocaine.

I was killing myself by bingeing nightly. What was I to do? I had spent thousands of dollars over the years trying new methods of weight loss. I took pills and injections to curb my appetite and nearly went psychotic. Nothing seemed to work for me. I understand now that those methods were unsuccessful because the problem was not only my physical weight. It was also the weight of my poor self-esteem.

The Wilderness

"Love yourself" was what the self-help books were telling me. I read many, and sometimes I would feel uplifted but would soon sink back into the depths of despair. I would be absent from as many social and family events as possible. Even when I would force myself to attend, it was not me they would encounter; it was the "normal" person I sent to represent me. I disappointed a lot of people that I really cared about, but nothing seemed to cause me to really make a change. I had become so good at pretending that I had no idea who I was or where I was going.

My romantic relationships always ended poorly because I was a fake from the beginning. There were always long intervals between my relationships. I would lose weight, become happy, and attract some interested party who would soon find that he had not gotten what he bargained for in this "normal" and intelligent woman.

I lived with one of my boyfriends for a while until he began to interfere with my food. I would go into a rage if he ate something that I had intended for myself. He was confused by my behavior and would calmly explain, "But you can just go buy some more!" In my crazed, addicted mind, that was a foolish idea. I wanted it now, I needed it now, and to interrupt my expectation of immediate gratification was unacceptable. He would just have to learn to stay out of my food. I was a hard nut to crack, as one of my recovery program counselors once remarked.

I was an intelligent person who was caught in the grips of a formidable enemy that could only be defeated by spiritual means. The journey was to begin by my admission that I had a problem that was more than "enjoying food." My behavior was making my life unmanageable, and I was suffering. It was the fatigue of fighting my disease that brought me to cry out in the wilderness for relief. I needed help, and I was ready to surrender in order to get it.

The decision to heal is a long way from the actual journey, but it was the start that I needed. I left my family and friends and went to an inpatient recovery program that dealt with eating disorders. I planned to stay for thirty days and ended up in treatment for an entire year.

I learned a lot during my time at "college," as we jokingly called the recovery program. I learned that all obese people are not food addicts. The food addict, like the drug addict, is a special breed of human being who has both an "allergy" (an abnormal and unquenchable physical reaction/craving for certain food substances); and a "mental obsession" that keeps her/him almost constantly focused on food.

There is no quick fix for food addiction, because the substance of choice is readily available everywhere. Imagine a drug addict finding a Thanksgiving dinner table full of pills, cocaine, and heroin waiting for her at Mom's house. My childhood traumas wreaked havoc on my addictive personality. However, it was most often my lack of understanding that allowed me to repeatedly re-trigger the traumas that hindered my life, liberty, and pursuit of happiness. In fact, for quite a while, life was just something I did between eating. I felt compelled to stuff down my feelings. There was nothing more frightening than to feel my feelings.

I am still on the long journey to recovery, one day at a time. I am committed to pressing on, no matter how long it takes. My life goal is to love myself unconditionally. Writing this wilderness testimony helps me to get to the core of my pain where the healing must take place. I am excited about what the future holds for me, and this is an indication that self-love has already begun to shine through.

The Light

I have not binged on food or other substances in more than seven years, but I still struggle with overeating. I still have the allergy that triggers me to crave more of certain foods. But I am slowly learning to make better and healthier food choices without feeling like I am punishing myself.

The mental obsession has, by the grace of God, been lifted. I no longer shut myself up and eat until I pass out. I no longer go out in the middle of the night looking for convenience stores and fast food shops. I do not hide food, and I share food with others without difficulty. That is amazing progress! I will continue on this journey of recovery because I know that I deserve the happiness it gives me. The light that I have found reveals that I am, and have always been, whole and complete. I am a spiritual being, and the real of me is perfect and powerful.

As a spiritual and biblical model, Hagar demonstrates that no matter what our present circumstances are, we should never give up. Hagar survived her trials in the wilderness and found light when she most needed it. We must continue to love ourselves no matter what. I invite you to join me as I continue this journey. Let us see ourselves as whole and complete, loving ourselves as God loves us—unconditionally.

I am learning to love myself more each day. And that, my beloved, is truly a brilliant light in the wilderness.

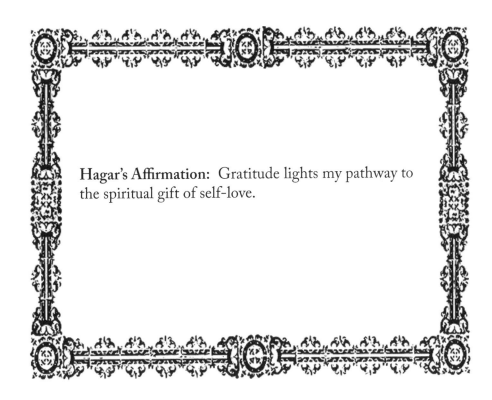

Hagar's Affirmation: Gratitude lights my pathway to the spiritual gift of self-love.

AFTERWORD

My sincere desire is that those who read these short stories that reflect challenging episodes in my life will feel some kinship and encouragement. Perhaps some of the words that arrived on these pages were especially meant for you.

I learned that we all have the capacity to overcome whatever circumstances we face in life. The comfort, encouragement, and reassurance that you may get from the sharing of these stories are worth more to me than gold. Please feel free to reflect on these experiences and how they may relate to your life stories. When you quietly and positively revisit your experiences, I believe that you will find that there was always someone, something, or a glimmer of light in the shadows of your emotional wilderness experiences.

You need never be afraid of life's twists and turns, because you can look at your own personal history and that of others who have faced adversity and overcome. Your light shines wherever you are and that includes those challenging moments in the wilderness of your mind.

One of the most important messages I want to leave with you is that you have enormous power to overcome any undesirable condition in your life. This and other soul-nourishing life lessons were taught to me by women who spoke their truth. My eternal gratitude flows to them all, especially: Rev. Robbie Sullivan, Rev. Dr. Mary A. Tumpkin, Rev. Shirley A. Aquart, Dr. Mary Watson and Ms. Mary Lou Allen. Now, I invite you to lean back, take a deep breath, and begin to understand that you are the Light in the Wilderness.

ABOUT THE AUTHOR

Dr. Patricia Darrah is a practitioner and teacher of metaphysics. She is dedicated to sharing the encouragement and inspiration she received from her gifted spiritual and lay teachers. Dr. Pat, as she is affectionately called, holds academic degrees in Psychology and Counseling, and a Doctorate in Psychoeducational Processes. She is a graduate of the Hagar's School of Mediumship and Psychology as were her mother and grandmother before her. She earned a Master's Certificate in Metaphysical Bible Studies at the Universal Truth Center in Miami Gardens, Florida. Two years ago, Dr. Pat founded a weekly teleconference called "The Power of Thought." She, along with a panel of other metaphysical thinkers, explores spiritual principles as they apply to practical life situations. Dr. Pat is a dynamic speaker and workshop facilitator. Her joy comes from helping others discover their inner light through learning and practicing truth principles. Dr. Pat is a native of Philadelphia, PA and currently resides in Washington, DC where she works as a Case Manager for the PATHS POWER Program at the University of the District of Columbia.